# Pieces of Water
## Reflections on Living in Light

Sarah Rhinelander

*Pieces of Water*
Copyright © 2019 Sarah Rhinelander

ISBN: 978-1-63381-175-1

*Artwork by Sarah Rhinelander*

All rights reserved. No part of this book may be reproduced in any form or by any electronic or mechanical means, including information storage and retrieval systems, without permission in writing from the author, except by a reviewer, who may quote brief passages in review.

*Designed and produced by:*
Maine Authors Publishing
12 High Street, Thomaston, Maine
www.maineauthorspublishing.com

Printed in the United States of America

Treat every task,
However mundane,

With focus and care.

All that you do
is sacred.

# Table of Contents

## Part I: Making God Soup

Making God Soup ................................................ 1
Let Me Be Foolish ............................................... 2
This Day ............................................................ 3
Five Things ........................................................ 4
Follow Me .......................................................... 5
The Not So Small Voice .................................... 6
Just Add Faith ................................................... 7
Praying 101 ....................................................... 8
Morning Prayer ................................................. 9
There Is No Lack ............................................. 10
Perfect ............................................................. 11
This Is It .......................................................... 12
Jackpot ............................................................ 13
Instant Gratification ........................................ 14
The Banquet .................................................... 15
Barn Doors ...................................................... 16
Stowaway ........................................................ 17
Let Things Get to You ..................................... 18
The Truth ........................................................ 19
See, Clearly ..................................................... 20
There by God .................................................. 21
Plan for No Disaster ....................................... 22
Do Right ......................................................... 23

Upset the Curve ................................................... 24
Full Up ................................................................ 25
Making Honey .................................................... 26
Let Things Be Light ............................................ 27
Get Ready ........................................................... 28
Live as Though ................................................... 29
The Most Simple Thing ...................................... 30

## Part II: Pieces of Water

Urgent ................................................................ 35
You Are Not Your Stuff ...................................... 36
Pieces of Water ................................................... 39
Badly Set Bones .................................................. 40
Crashing Down Days .......................................... 41
Good Things ....................................................... 42
Toast ................................................................... 43
Grumpy .............................................................. 44
Smart People ...................................................... 45
Up and Down ..................................................... 46
Teeter .................................................................. 47
As Within ........................................................... 48
The Greatest Revolution .................................... 49
Whitewall ........................................................... 50
We Cannot Stand Against It .............................. 51
Your Other Heart ............................................... 52
See Thoughts Through ....................................... 54
Happy ................................................................. 55

Easy ................................................................ 56
What a World ................................................. 57
I Ask Some Questions ...................................... 58
Negatives ........................................................ 60
What If? .......................................................... 61
Sweet .............................................................. 62
Your Daily Practice ......................................... 63
Emancipation ................................................. 64
Unexpect ........................................................ 65
All of It ........................................................... 66
Soul Flyer ....................................................... 68
Perishable ....................................................... 69

## Part III: Animals

Hank ............................................................... 72
Miracles .......................................................... 74
Heron ............................................................. 76
Big Hill ........................................................... 78
The Chicken Problem .................................... 79
Worthless ........................................................ 81
Schoolyard ...................................................... 83
From a Veranda .............................................. 84
Truce .............................................................. 85
Limpet ............................................................ 86
Witness ........................................................... 88
Fascia .............................................................. 89
Dead Someday ................................................ 90

Fish ............................................................... 92
This Is for the Birds ............................................ 94
Sister ............................................................... 96
Sunsound ........................................................ 100
Ice Fishing ...................................................... 101
Lion ................................................................ 103
Wonder ........................................................... 104
Soap Bubble .................................................... 105
Old Coat ......................................................... 106
Baton .............................................................. 107
What is Left .................................................... 109
These Things I See ........................................... 110
Big Bed ........................................................... 112
Animals ........................................................... 113
Old Hen .......................................................... 118

# Part I
# Making God Soup

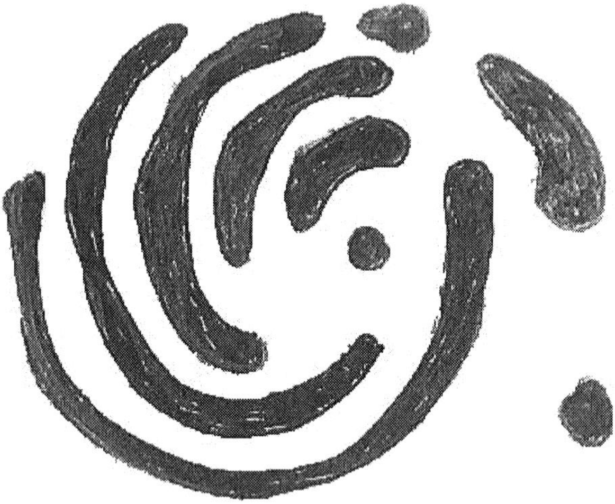

# Making God Soup

What does your life desire?
This soup lacks something.

What is it that your tongue wants to taste?
Find it in your cupboard.

Add it in, just a smidge.
Taste it.

Is that it?
Not quite.

Try again.
A little different.

Aha.
There it is.

This is what my soup wants.
This is what my life desires.

# Let Me Be Foolish

Let me be foolish today
And authentic.
Let me set down my false modesty, my arrogance,

My cherished belief
In all the things I Know For Sure,
That I Am Good At,

The Things That I Cannot Be Taught.
Let me keep my mouth shut.
Let me be a student of life.

Let me put all others above me
As teachers.
Today let me be foolish,

Happy and peaceful.
Today let me be generous
With my laughter,
With my foolishness.

# This Day

This is your day today:

In this day,
There is the perfect
Amount of time.

People are
Exactly
As they should be.

Accept them,
And yourself,
Without reservation.

See the abundance in this day
And open toward it.
Accept your abundance with open arms.

Let this day
Be perfect and bright.

# Five Things

1. The path is eternal.
2. Everything is the path.
3. You are always on the path.
4. You cannot lose your way.
5. Knowing this helps.

# Follow Me

Go deeper into your faith.
Get lost in it.
Let everyone think you are crazy.
Let everyone say it is time to grow up,
To be serious, to get real.
Let them say that it will never work.
Let them all say these things.
Be kind and gracious and humble in yourself.
Laugh at yourself, right along with them.
Keep your head down.
Keep on working.
Do what is right. You know what that is.
See what happens.
And when it comes to be,
Say, "Look what happened!"
Not in a gloating,
"I told you so" way.
But in a way that says,

"Come on!
  Come on!
    Come on!

      Follow me!"

# The Not So Small Voice

Finding
That small, still voice-
It is not small,
It is not still.

This voice sings out loud.
It waves its arms.
It shouts.
It dances!

This voice is vibrant
And strong.
This voice will move you
In ways you never thought that you could move.

It will make you as a kid again.
It will shout the magic back into your life.
Let it not be still,
Let it not be small.

# Just Add Faith

If you just add faith
To the mix:

Impatience is anticipation.
Obstacles are challenges.
Sadness is warm memory.
Craving is motivation.
Anger is the energy for change.
Envy shows you what you want.
Emptiness is a time to rest.
Frustration with others is a mirror.
Doubt strengthens faith.
In loneliness you befriend yourself.
The past teaches.
The future is friendly.

The present is
Your home.

# Praying 101:

Don't say please.

Say thank you.

## Morning Prayer

May I find
What is right in this day
And follow it.

May I have an open heart today
And compassion for all beings.

Today, may I be
Even more humble
And grateful

Than I was
Yesterday.

# There Is No Lack

There is no lack.

There is life.
There is love.
There is the power
And the pace
Of change.
There are spaces
Into which
You may grow.

There is no lack.

## Perfect

Belief
Makes your world as it is.

As you believe,
So shall your world be.

All is perfect.

Your belief
Is the only thing

Keeping you
From this perfection.

## This Is It

This is what it is
To be alive.

This is
All there is.

This
Is everything.

# Jackpot

Wealth does not always
Bring gratitude,

But gratitude
Always brings wealth.

# Instant Gratification

Your prayers have already
Been answered.

If you open your eyes to see,
You will know that this is true.

Everything is an answer
To your prayer,

Whether you remember the prayer
Or not.

Be overwhelmed by your blessings.

No prayer
Goes unanswered.

## The Banquet

You have laid a lavish table
That would make me overfull.

Let me be satisfied and amazed.
Let me have my fill
And not be greedy.

Let me not regret
What I could not take in.

Let me be always thankful.
Let me never
Take another meal
For granted.

## Barn Doors

Open your barn doors wide
To all that is outside of you.

Everything will come in:
The dust, the perfume, the pollen,
The light and the rain.

Receive and accept all, equally.

The only difference
Between pleasure and pain

Is held in your doors
That keep you from the world.

## Stowaway

You hold your peace within you.
If you cannot find peace
In yourself,
Where you are right now,
You could move to the ends of the earth,
And still
You would not find it.

You hold your peace within you.
If you can find peace
In yourself,
Where you are right now,
You can move to the ends of the earth,
And still
Your peace
Will find you.

# Let Things Get to You

Let things get to you,
An un-cloistered monk.
Unshielded from the ugly winds.

Let things blow through you
And away.

When the storm has passed,
Stay steady
In your kindness.

# The Truth

Though the world is dangerous,
You are safe.

Though the world is filled with anguish,
You are joyful.

In the midst of violence,
You are at peace.

Though you are connected to all others,
You are alone here on earth.

Though you are alone here,
You are never alone in spirit.

Believe in yourself,
And you believe in God.

# See, Clearly

See
Through fear.
See that it is an illusion.

See
Through loss.
See that it is an illusion.

See
Through craving.
See that it is an illusion.

See
That you cannot be harmed,
That there is nothing to lose,
That there is nothing you need.

See that all is illusion.

See, clearly,
That there is,
Literally,
Nothing to fear.

# There by God

When you have exhausted
All of your answers,
And are left

With only questions,
Then you have
Your answer.

And there,
By God,
You are.

# Plan for No Disaster

Prepare for
Improvement.

Get ready for
Impending joy.

Get your adventure kit
Ready.

Get ready
For good things.

## Do Right

Get to know how right feels.
What you are doing at this moment

Is what you will continue to do,
Unless you change it.

So catch yourself
Sooner and sooner

When you are doing
Not quite the right thing,

And do right instead.
Keep on doing this,

Over and over,
Until doing right

Is the only thing
You do.

This is how you change
For good.

## Upset the Curve

Change.
Be unpredictable.
Be unreasonably successful.
Upset the curve.
Ruin dire predictions of failure.
Surprise people.
Surprise yourself.

# Full Up

If you live your life fully,
There is no space for discontent.

There is reveling in the success of others
As much as your own.

There is connection and grace,
Peace and love.

There is no room left
For anything else.

# Making Honey

Your heart holds the truth
Of your desire.

Your mind is a tool
Used to broadcast your desire.

Your body is the strength
That brings your desire to form.

You are a worker bee,
Manifesting.

## Let Things Be Light

You don't need to brace
For impending disaster.
You can expect a good outcome.

You are safe.

So relax.
Anticipate good.
Let things be light.

## Get Ready

For the rest of your life,
Get ready to
Die.
Get your affairs in order.
Don't leave a mess for anyone to clean up.
Take care
        of all loose ends.
Finish
        all of the projects that are worth your while.
Say
        the things that you need to say.
Do
        your most important work well.
Love
        everyone that you can possibly love.
Be yourself.
        and be at peace with that.
Be young
        until the very last breath.
Get done
        as much as you can here before you leave.
Be good
        and ready for your departure.

At your death,
Be ready
To go.

# Live as Though

Live as though
You are demonstrating a life fully lived.

Live as though
You are showing what integrity means.

Make your life self evident
In its honesty.

Be the most steadfast
In your purpose.

Do not lecture others.
Know your faults,

Know also that you are blind to most of them.
Let this knowledge keep you steady and humble
always.

Live as though
You know you are alive.

# The Most Simple Thing

What is the simplest thing?
When you reduce everything to its essence-
What is left?

When you take away all else,
You find the simplicity of here,
Of now.

Here and now is never ending joy,
Not just within your reach,
But within you.

Only here,
Only now.
Never ending joy.

Spreading, flowering
In the shower of your attention.

This is the simplest thing.

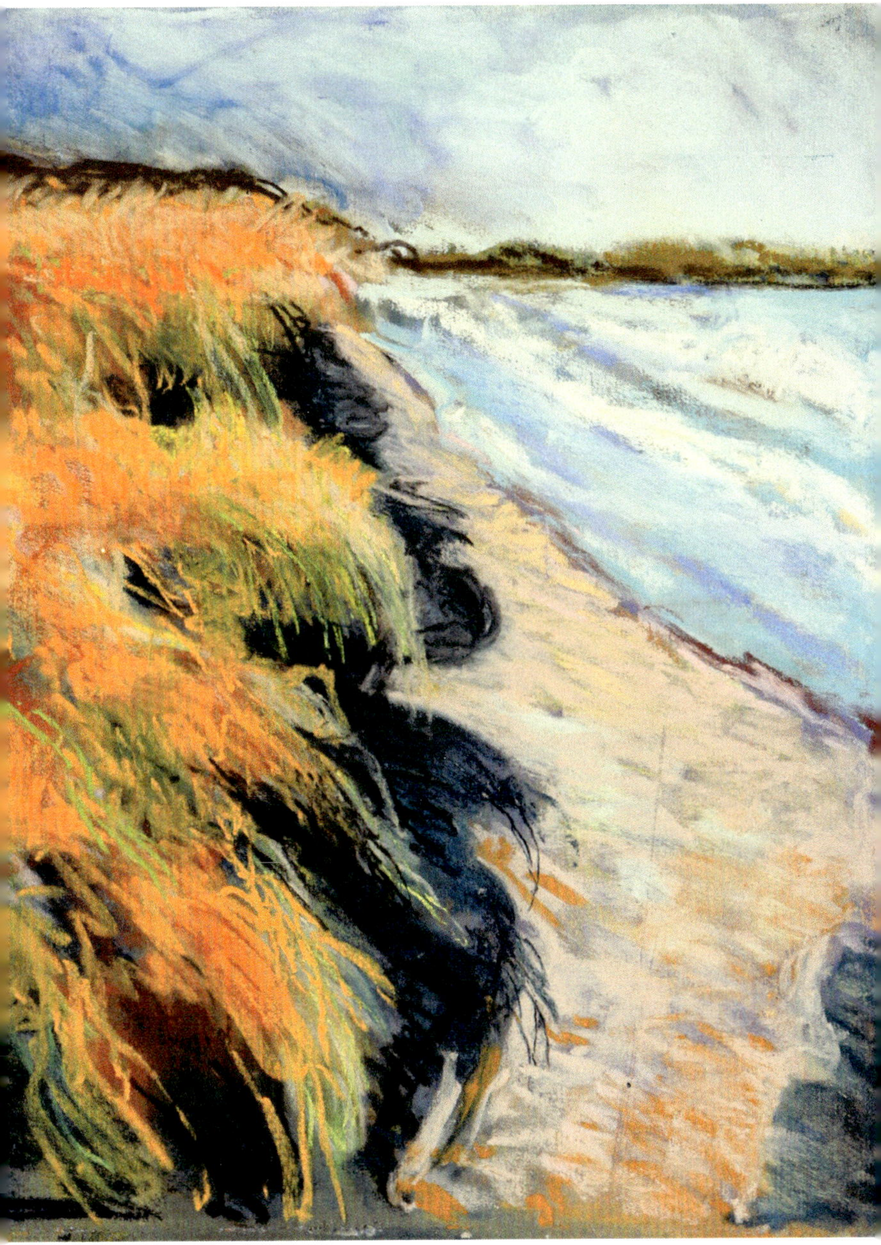

## Part II
# Pieces of Water

ABSORBING
THE LIGHT

# Urgent

There is
No more time
For separation
From love.

# You Are Not Your Stuff

You are not your stuff.
You are not your
Smart talk.
You are not you
At your best moment.

What you are
Is a chair
That God sits in for a while
To see what the view is like
From down here.

God sits in you
To see the world,
To feel the world
Through your eyes,
Through your fingers.

To feel
What hair feels like,
What a breeze feels like,
And what scarce
February feels like

With her still cold sunlight
That burns through all of
Your deceptions
Of yourself.

You are not your stuff.

38

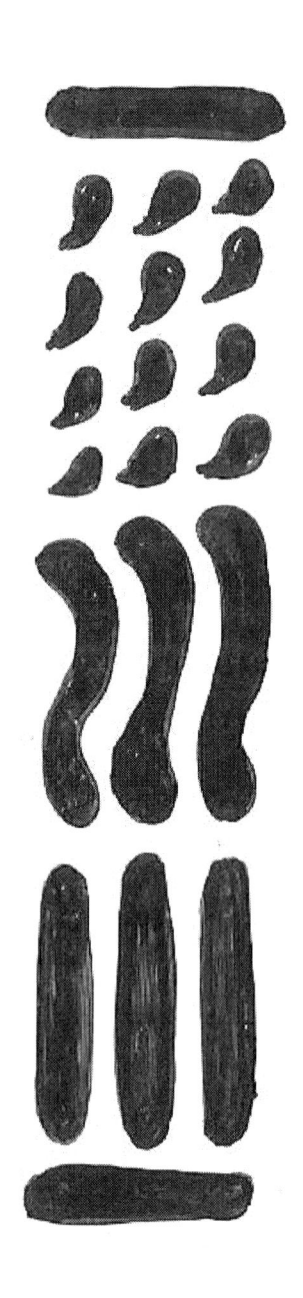

# Pieces of Water

Peace be with you.
Peace be with me.
Let me have what I need.
Let you have what you need.
Both of us.
Let there not be a winning side.
Let it settle out as the ocean does,
With waves that break
And recede
And break again.
Let us not hold back the tide
Or force it ahead of its time.
Let us let go of any divisions
Between you and me.
Let us be equal
Like two pieces of water
In the same ocean.

## Badly Set Bones

We have
Some badly set bones.

We are being re-broken

So that we may finally
Mend right.

# Crashing Down Days

These crashing down days,
Where you can feel
Even your bones drooping,
Are not just days to get through.

Before pills and light bulbs and television,
You humans would in winter
Sink low in the darkest days
And learn of yourself at your very least,
Blind to the sun and shadowless
As the sun is, for a time, blind to you.

You know that you will come back up,
You always do,
Like a frog from his chilly bed
In spring sun blinking.
So do not hasten hibernation.

Instead, in this long night, stay sunk.
Frog-paddle through your ancient mud
And find the lumps and fossils
That hold the truth of who you really are
When there is nothing bright about you.

# Good Things

A good thing
Just happened.

Find it.
Notice it.
Be happy about it.

A good thing
Just happened.

This is always
Always
Always
True.

# Toast

Conversations
In your mind

Are a waste
Of your mind.

So tap your glass,
Let it ring out

In a room of
Quieting crystal.

This is the nice way,
The polite way,

To say to your eager,
Murmuring crowd,

Shut up
And listen.

# Grumpy

You will never be

More self-righteous,

More defensive,

Or more grumpy

Than when

First faced

With the truth

Of yourself.

# Smart People

We are all
Very intelligently
Held apart.

We are all too sophisticated
To be
Taken in.

We are savvy and cynical.
None of us
Are fools.

We all
Talk
A good line.

Only love
Makes us
Dumb.

# Up and Down

As deep down as you dig
Into your earth


You rise up
Into your sky.

# Teeter

On the shaky ground
Of your defenses,
Your coy ways
Topsy-turvy,
Always working
Flailing your arms,
Balanced on the narrow gauge
Of your beliefs,
Your hostility
In keeping
Yourself defended:
Fall.
Alight.
Befriend.
Your tightrope becomes
A broad and level walkway
Lined
With smooth and sacred
Stones.

# As Within

Neaten your mind.
The world around you
Will align,
Neaten.

Simplify your mind.
Your life will simplify.

Clear your mind.
Your life will settle
Into a clear and pleasant
Course.

# The Greatest Revolution

Would be
If we all suddenly
Started doing
Our Art,
Our Music,
Our Craft,
Our Passion,
The thing we love
The best
Full tilt.
No holds barred.
To hell with everything else.
This would be the greatest revolution.
The shackles would fall away.
Wars,
Advertisements,
Lobbyists,
Diets,
Retirement,
And Prozac
Would no longer work.

Wouldn't that just
Be the day?

# Whitewall

Peace is behind all things.
A white wall on which
Violence is written
And erased.

Peace is behind all things.
Feel it in the
White walls
Of your bones.

# We Cannot Stand Against It

A soft surrounding
Velvet

Ensnares and invades us,
Wearing down our steely hold

On every looming terrible deed,
Every small mean stupid moment,

So that they finally slip our grasp
And we become the secret happy people

Who can love others
Wholly and unhidden.

Insidious, forgiveness pries us
From our greedy brokenness.

Inevitable, it fixes all
Less-than-perfect things.

# Your Other Heart

When you feel pain-
Anger, sorrow, fear:
Don't swallow it
Or throw it at another.

Instead,
Look at it.
There it is:
A silver orb, spinning.

Pewter,
Whisking off in tendrils.
It stops, it hovers,
Just outside yourself.
A winter heart.

You can make pain heavy
Like a wrecking ball,
Or you can make it a bright and
Dancing ball
Of mercurial light.

You can be with it,
Marvel at it,
Feel its texture,

Then pass through it.
Like tasting
        the color
                of air.

# See Thoughts Through

See

Every thought
Through
To its transparency.

Every single
Thing
You know is true

Is not.

# Happy

Find the thing
In your life
That makes
All else
Peripheral.

Find the thing
In your life
That resounds in you
And spills over
In the highest vibration
Of your happy soul,
Reverberating
In a joyful crescendo
Of creation.

Do the thing
In your life
That makes
The Creator in you,
The God in you,
Happy.

# Easy

On the other side
Of manipulation

Is wanting love.
As simple as the sky.

How cruel we can be
In our craving for kindness.

How cold we become
Toward those who warm us.

What depths we sink to
As we lever for the highest thing.

How complicated
We make things.

If we only knew
How easy it really is:

You see,
Love is in the air around us.

To get it
All we have to do

Is breathe.

## What a World

What a world
It would be
If we all lived our truth.

What a ruckus there would be to start!
And then, how good things
Would start to happen.

How admiring and supportive we would be
Of one another, with nothing to resent.
Imagine a world without resentment:

Aligning,
Synchronizing,
All working together in the Great Symphony.

Your truth
Is the greatest gift
You give the world.

Live your truth.
Be brave enough
To do that.

# I Ask Some Questions

What is real?
The journey is real.

What should I do?
What keeps you in the moment with your heart open.

Who is my teacher?
No-one and everyone.

What shall I let go?
The things that numb you.

What shall I cherish?
The things that disarm you.

Whom shall I be with?
Those who make you laugh.

Why am I sad?
Because you are not here.
You are in the past.

Why am I fearful?
Because you are not here.
You are in the future.

Why do I crave?
Because you are not here,
Where your innermost self wishes to be.

How do I live?
With your body, mind and spirit aligned
In the grand and simple purpose
Of being fully present.

What should I love?
Life and all that is in it.

Who is with me?
All fellow journeyers,
Just like you.

# Negatives

My heart is as open as the sky,
Without fear.
With fear,
My heart is a raisin,
Shriveled and protected.
This monster mirage,
Imagined hurts of the future,
The ways I might not win,
The things I hold as true about me
Threatened,
Or so I think.
These dire consequences,
This grave danger,
Based on negatives of the past:
If I wiped this silver plate clean
I could start anew
With fresh mercury,
And love again
With a heart
The size of the sky.

May I?

## What If?

What if you defend your dreams

As fiercely

As you do your excuses?

## Sweet

There is a funny thing
That I never knew
Before.

To give up the struggle,
Every last defense,
Is a sacrifice.

Like eating an ice cream sundae
With everything on it
Is a sacrifice.

This awful, awful thing,
That I struggled, at all costs,
To avoid.

This dreaded,
Delightful
Dessert.

# Your Daily Practice

When your daily practice has become
As regular as breathing,

Let it overtake your day.
When you are confused and conflicted,

Find that place where there is nothing.
Fall into it. Just for a moment.

Know how much God loves you.
Feel the Lion's warm breath.

Let your daily practice
Overtake your day.

Let your daily practice
Become who you are.

# Emancipation

There is a life you live in your head.
You know the one I mean. A life in the future.
A perfect life, a fair life, a life where you
Have all that you don't like to do, done.
Where you have it all figured out,
And have everything you want,
And have got it all together,
And do everything well,
And look good doing it.
A life that starts
Tomorrow.
A life
That
Is
A bar
Across a window
That keeps you from this life.
You know the one I mean. This life,
With all the projects never quite done.
This life, where you don't yet have all you want.
This life, with wrinkled clothes and ketchup stains.
This life, where you screw up, fall down, and are a jerk.
This life, that is so much better than that life in your head.
Because in this life, surprising, unpredictable things happen,
Wonderful things that you can't yet possibly know.
Because in this life,
You are actually
Here,
Living.

# Unexpect

Don't expect perfection.
Don't expect
What you
Expect.

Expect, instead, all faults,
All mistakes.
Expect others to be just as you are,
Flawed and searching.

Then
Be surprised,
Be blessed,
With goodness.

# All of It

Forgive.
This is what the old woman says.
The one on my death bed.
The one with my eyes.

She says,
Forgive every moment.
Don't base your life, any of it,
On old wounds, old hurts.
There is no injustice.
There is only what is now.

Love and use your body,
Because I know first hand
That you will not always have it.
Use your strength.
Marvel and revel in it.

Love and use your mind
Even when it is crowded and anguished.
Follow your strongest loves
Even when you know
They will destroy you.

Make your dreams.
You will be startled
And pleased by them
Much sooner than you think.

All others, all things,
Are your teachers.
So be quiet and listen.

The only regret,
This old woman says,
Would be in not trying,
Not learning,
Not loving
All that you could,
All of it,

      All of it,

           When you had
                The chance.

# Soul Flyer

Your soul flies
Out over the ocean.
Under the cold stars,
Far above the circling earth,
In a wide wide sky.

All you know of it
Is the tug, the vibration,
The string.
This hum, this tension
That gets all things done.

When you are finished here,
Your kite will fly free
Of being a soul,
Up, up, up,
Dancing, joining,
And joyous.

# Perishable

You can always love more.
There is no saving it up.

It will not run out.
You cannot

Keep love
Un-given.

# Part III
# Animals

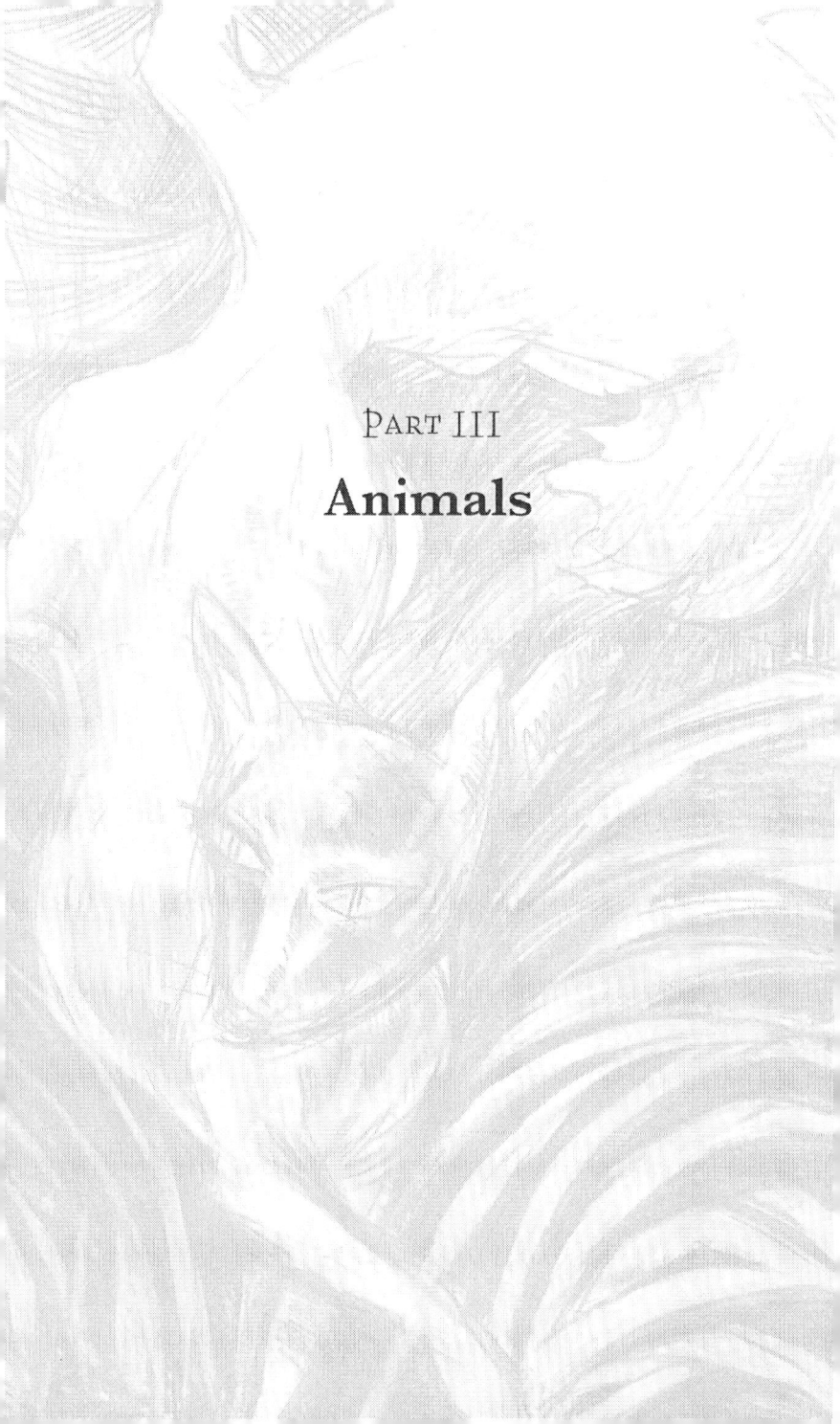

# Hank

I have a dog
Who wanders.
He lets himself out
Through a hole in the fence,
And takes himself
For a walk.
He goes joggling down the road
On his porky corgi legs,
Single-purposed,
Relaxed.
A while later
He comes back,
Creaks his way
Through the push gate,
And takes his place
In the sandpit
Under the porch,
Doing his job,
Guarding the chickens.
Why, then, does he wander?
Just to remind himself that he can,
That he is only 90 percent domestic,
With a part
That still wakens
To the wild world
Outside the fence,
Getting into a little trouble,

Maybe a scrap now and then
If it comes to that,
And when he is ready
   (not before)
Returning home
To do his good dog duty
Keeping us safe,
Secretly satisfied
Knowing that he is still
Just a little bit
Free.

# Miracles

Now I say thank you
Thank you thank you
A thousand times a day
To the universe
For this amazing life.
Instantly
Synchronicity
Crashes into me
In some quirky funny way
And I get winded
From the force
Of these ridiculously
Over-the-top
Miracles.
Now they happen so often
That I plan for them
And wonder what new thing
Will happen perfectly today.
I now realize
This is simply
The normal everyday
Process of the universe

Saying
A thousand times a day
You are most entirely
Welcome.

# Heron

Heron,
When he is fishing
On his long spare legs,
Ringed with water and with weeds,
Is intent and slow
Yet he moves
Perfectly
Like a machine
Of grace and awareness.
He is not worried
About not catching something.
He is just there,
Scoping through with
His sideways eyes,
His grey blue dusty body
Shifting,
A gymnast
Ready.
Seeing.
Stopping.

And then

Still.

Still.

Still.

For as long as it takes

To get what he wants.

# Big Hill

I ride my bicycle
Almost every day these days,
And I am a kid again.
It saves me.

There is one big hill
That grabs me every time,
By the hand,
Like another kid,
Grinning and whooping

As we race on down
Around the curve,
Hair and thoughts blown back,
Tempting fate,

Loving gravity,
As the earth pulls us,
Flies us
Toward its molten core.

# The Chicken Problem

I get it now.
I see why we resist
Seeing all as sacred and connected:
Once you see the world this way,
You can no longer see it otherwise.
It is so obvious,
So gorgeous.

My problem, however,
Is with the chickens.
Those sacred chickens,
Crammed into factory farms,
Forced to lay their sacred eggs
For all of us
Sacred people.

I find that my newly opened heart
Baulks
At feeling what they feel, these,
My fellow, captive creatures.

To dissolve every cruel tiny cage,
In breezy green fields, heavy with grubs,
With dust baths and shady trees for napping.
To let them live by their own design,

Not ours,
This would be the right thing.

But the cages stand strong,
Glaringly wrong.
And my heart baulks
And breaks.

So this business
Of living with an open heart,
Connecting to all creatures,
Would be a whole lot easier
If it weren't for
The chickens.

# Worthless

Moss grows on a rock
That is worth no money.
It is just a rock
And on it moss grows,
Wiry and humble.

Moss,
When I, so heavy and unthinking, step there,
Gives way, and it wakes me
From my dull nature
To its lively nature

And I change my course.

For the shallow roots
With nothing to hold them up
Or down,
Needing no ground
For life, puritan
And persistent,
Are much more precious

Than my decided way.

This lovely soft moss
That wakes me,

That I could have as a bed,
Needs only this dull rock to grow.
So now I am thinking

That to change course

And make a garden
Where things grow well,
Cannot be that difficult
When just a rock,
Worth no money at all,
Produces such
Tender, strong,
Liberating
Life.

# Schoolyard

The first open-window evening
In Maine.
Such a startling, smiling sound
After the muffling of winter.
What a happy racket!

So what do they holler about?
Being born? The cold water?
Are they like the baby penguins?
Each peeper with a frantic call
That brings momma hopping?
No, I don't think so.

I imagine instead
They are a herd of rowdy kids
Let out at recess,
Shoving through the door,
Shoulder to tadpole shoulder, yelling,

"SPRING! SPRING! SPRING! SPRING! SPRING!"

Each out-shouting the other
From tiny shiny bodies,
In a joyous frenzy
Of fresh new existence.

# From a Veranda

If you think
That God might be talking to you,

God probably is,

Through the circus clouds
And the crazy blue of the ocean,

Sincere smiles
And busting-out laughter,

The kind that turns heads,
Makes people turn and glare,

Which is, of course,
The best kind.

# Truce

Find your humor,
Porcupine.
Surrender your bristling,
Your circling,
Displaying your
Impressive backside.
I am chastened, and concede:
Your weaponry is superior.

So soften those black-bean eyes
From under that cantankerous brow.
Lay down your quills
And figure-eight away
As only you can,
In the circular motion
Of your sturdy muscled legs.

That done,
Wearing once again your
Benign and handsome tweed,
You are ever
A wise warrior
Of peace.
Now, on to the next thing.
Looking for bark.

# Limpet

I am being pried
From my pride,

Like a child from her
Favorite toy.

Incredulous,
Wailing and indignant.

I am being pried
From who I am

To become only
A small sharp shard

In this great glass world
That sparkles,

Surrounds,
And permeates.

I am being pried from
The prison of me.

After my tantrum,
Petulance, a fantastic sulk,

In the first faint shimmer
Of my final defeat

A burning,

Beautiful,

Blinding

Light.

# Witness

Thoughts
Have space around them.

They don't take up the whole horizon.

Thoughts are globlets
Swimming on sunlit eyelids.

They fall apart
To make space.

I used to be scared.
Now, curious.

Crow watches.

Bright eyed,
Amused.

Seeing me see.

# Fascia

This silver whispering web
That criss-crosses
Around and inside of me
Glistening and beautiful
Lets me move and
Sleep and do my work,
And extends outside of me
In tendrils of silent
Light and waves
Of sound and weaving thought,
And explores out through
The prismed branches of the trees
That make a mosaic
Of the pieces of sky,
Reaching out and
Even further in to
Build the silver walls
That bridge the worlds
Between and around us,
Twining their pattern
Of shimmering threads
That forever tie together
The very innermost
Of you and me
And everything.

# Dead Someday

You will be dead someday.
Yes, you.
I know you don't want to think about it.
But after your grimace,

Resist the urge to think of other, lighter things.

Stay, instead
In this discomfort,
And befriend it.

Make it a game, a challenge:
How much can you see,
How much can you do,
In the time you have left?
What things matter?
And what do not?

The end of your journey
Is already in you.
So feel yourself finite,
Mortal and ethereal,
Fleeting and strong.

Every day, hone your life
To its essentials.
Everything not on your journey
Let it go.

"I will be dead someday."

Repeat these words
Every day,
Until you know them well,
Until they carry you
Over that deep trench of dread,
Into the dawning, dazzling land
Of being fully alive.

# Fish

As a fish is

To the ocean

You are

To love.

So swim.

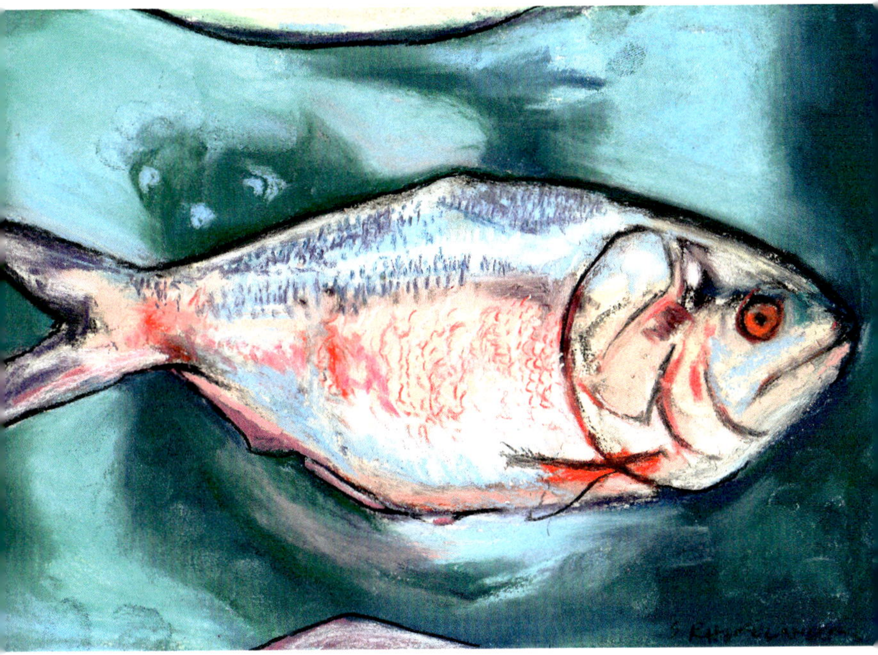

# This Is for the Birds

So what do I care
If a wild bird eats out of my hand?
I sit for a whole ninety seconds.

      The drama of it all wears thin.

My feet are cold.
My coffee cup is way over there.

Should I move?
Will I lose all that I have gained

      Sitting still?

I want so much to
Have a story to tell,
The trajectory of my day
Launched
By these tiny feathered things.

My efforts at nonchalance are like praying.
Pretending that I don't need,
Pretending that I don't want.
But my desire broadcasts itself:

It is only when I dump my handful of seed
And clump inside, grumbling
That I have more important things to do,
That the chirpers flock and stutter,

And light happily
Where I was just sitting.
I can't help but laugh.

    They see through me so perfectly.

## Sister

I dreamed the other night
That Jesus had a sister,
And that she was a funny
Irreverent girl.

She was there
To play jokes on Him,
To tell Him to lighten up,
And remind Him
That Life is, after all,
Just life.

She was not
In awe of him.
Jesus was just her
Holier than thou
Little brother.

She was his guide,
Well seated
In the earth:
Mortal, a clown,
Steady and wise.

Once, she turned
The wine back into water.
She grinned as he frowned
Over his rough wooden bowl,
And then said, innocently,
"…What?"

His sister was a pain
In Jesus's ass.
She would not let him
Take himself
Too seriously,

Even when all of
His disciples
Encouraged Him
To do just that.

Jesus needed her
To remind him
That humanity is God,
God is humanity,
And that these are the same.

The two grew older.
She watched him emerge,
Decide on his hard course,
And pass her by.
She was proud of him.

Then she was left behind.
She was wise enough
To let him go,
To understand.

Her love
Was the last of his sight.
Her good sense
Held him, comforted,
On the cross.

The echo
Of her easy laughter
Carried him through
His suffering.

In my dream
It was the best love,
A sister's love.
Selfless and fine.
A love that
Does not waver.

# Sunsound

If you are tangled
In a past moment,

Taken by someone, something,
Handed to a flame,

If sharpness catches you,
And you are outside yourself,
Powerless:

Listen

For the sound of the sun,
The voice of the universe

The Great Vibration,
Your heart hum.

The resonant tether
That hand over hand,

Brings you back
To yourself.

# Ice Fishing

The ice remembers.

Our ground is gone
But our footprints are held
In the soft dark water
Of summer.

Next year we are back
In the giant quiet
Of a frozen day.
The eagles high-wheel
Our fishing holes, hungry, patient,
Waiting for us to leave.

The ice circles us
With the memory
Of our deep-sleeping survivor,
Our latent adventurer,
Lulled and drugged
By the temperate ease of summer,

Now wakened by winter's first
Sharp-catching breath.
The fierce thrill

Of walking once again
On water.

Spring brings
The death of ice,
But the ice will keep you,
For you,

With blue-cold mercy,
The ice reformed,
You reborn,
Into a new winter,
A new day.

# Lion

Lion comes for me
Between wake and sleep
Rumbling like stones
On the ocean floor.

There is a storm above.
But here below,
In the shifting
Shafts of green,
We are safely
Cradled,

Tossed and tumbled
By love's
Wild
Tides.

# Wonder

God's gift to you
Is your heart of childhood
Kept whole.

Amazement kept alive.
Wonder, somehow preserved.
A heart stronger
But still young.

How can this be,
With so many hearts
Hardened,
Shattered?

How can this be?
It is yet another
Great thing
Of wonder.

## Soap Bubble

I used to live
In a soap bubble.

A sphere of iridescence
A pretty thing,

But delicate.

Disintegrating in a breath of air
Or a poked finger.

But with persistence,
And some help,

My bubble is tougher now,
No less beautiful,

A bouncing ball.
I float in here weightless,

Careen off the soft walls,
Laughing.

I sleep here,
Cradled in round and round,

In my safety
Dreaming.

## Old Coat

I wear love well now,
Like an old pea coat

With well-wandered
Softened threads.

Love has worn me well,
Like an old sea stone

Rolled and wandering,
All rough edges rounded.

# Baton

Give me your misery.
Let me take it from you,
To pass on
To one who needs it more,
To start their journey
As you have finished yours.

Though they know not where they are going,
Or even that there is a journey at all,
You know now
What they yet do not.
How tragedy's dark alchemy
Rolls you out of yourself,
Reduced to your very essence.
Lesser, but not less than.
Instead, rid of all not needed.

I know of misery's familiar comfort,
Its perfect knowledge of you.
The soft warm bed of sympathy
Where your great loss
Forgives all lapses,
All shortcomings.

But misery is finished with you.
It is time to open to your new self.

To breathe the clear cool air of grace.
To be once again measured
By what you make happen,
Not by what has happened to you.

So give me your misery.
Let me pass it on
To one who needs it more,
To start their journey
As you have finished yours.

## What is Left

And this
Is what I am.

Left,
After everything,

With strengths,
And a hole.

Like a missing tooth,
The gap

Where God
Gets in.

# These Things I See

God does not show himself
To those who are pious, or pray a lot,
Or those who are very good.

God shows himself to those who have,
By accident or on purpose,
Gone quiet.

We have driven him
Deep into the Old Forest.
Our static gets to him.

He just wants a quiet place to be
For a while.
So if you go into the Old Forest,
And sit at the dark base of the oldest tree,

And keep quiet and still
For a long, long time,
God may peek out

From a mossy hollow.
If you stay still enough,
Quiet enough,

God may tiptoe out
From the underbelly of the big pines
On long spindly legs.

He may stand in front of you,
Curious, a little shy,
But pleased to finally

Have a chance
To show Himself
To His creation.

# Big Bed

I now have
An odd tiny family
Of cast-away dogs
And patched-up people.
On cranky Monday mornings
We scowl around each other
Until we remember to laugh
And kiss goodbye.
But the best is this:
Each night, we leap, all of us,
Furry and not so furry,
Into our big bed
And we sleep,
Sometimes fitfully,
Sometimes dead as logs,
With a hand on a leg,
Or a head on a paw,
Sighing and slumbering,
Touching and not.
This tiny odd family
Meets every need,
Which is very simple.
We are resigned to happiness,
Despite everything.
We are no longer alone
And wandering.

# Animals

Like a child asleep
In the jungle,
I dream of animals.

Bats flash
In and out of firelight
Above a deep-gold field
Under star-filled skies.
I dance below them
As owl, yellow-eyed,
Waits and watches.

White Horse comes to me
Glowing with infinite colors,
Bringing silent lessons
Of fire and creation.
His face holds all the faces
That ever were,
That ever will be,
In a shifting, flickering,
Brilliant light.

Crow is always there
As I wake
With his blue-black eye
Witnessing my foolishness,
Forever entertained.

Hawk hovers,
Sways, far above, and finds for me
The path that winds among
The high mountains,
Shows me my lowly way
That I could not see
Without his higher sight.

Lion, with his huge love,
Comes rumbling.
In his heavy paws he cradles
The universe.
The top of my head
Opens like a lid,
And Lion takes me through it
On a soaring journey,
Racing, flying, through
The swirling stars
Of every galaxy.
He chuckles
At my small and worried mind
And shows me
Not to fear.

Bear now pads
Beside my path
Among the trees
With thick curved claws,
Noble and lumbering,
Graceful and practical
A father with small dark eyes.

Fawn is a child
Wide-eyed and trusting.

Wolf protects her.

Lynx tore me apart,
Dismembered me,
Before I knew my way.
She is now a lethal,
Quiet companion
Shielding my new,
Unfettered self.

But the very first was Seal.
He lolls on sun-warmed rocks
With his drooping, watery whiskers
And laughing chocolate eyes.
Rolls, slippery,
Into the water,
Teaching me
To play.

I dream of animals so often
Now they pad and fly,
Hop and slither
Out of the murky marsh of dream,
Over the fragile edge of sleep
Into my waking world.

Now all of my old dogs
Are with me.

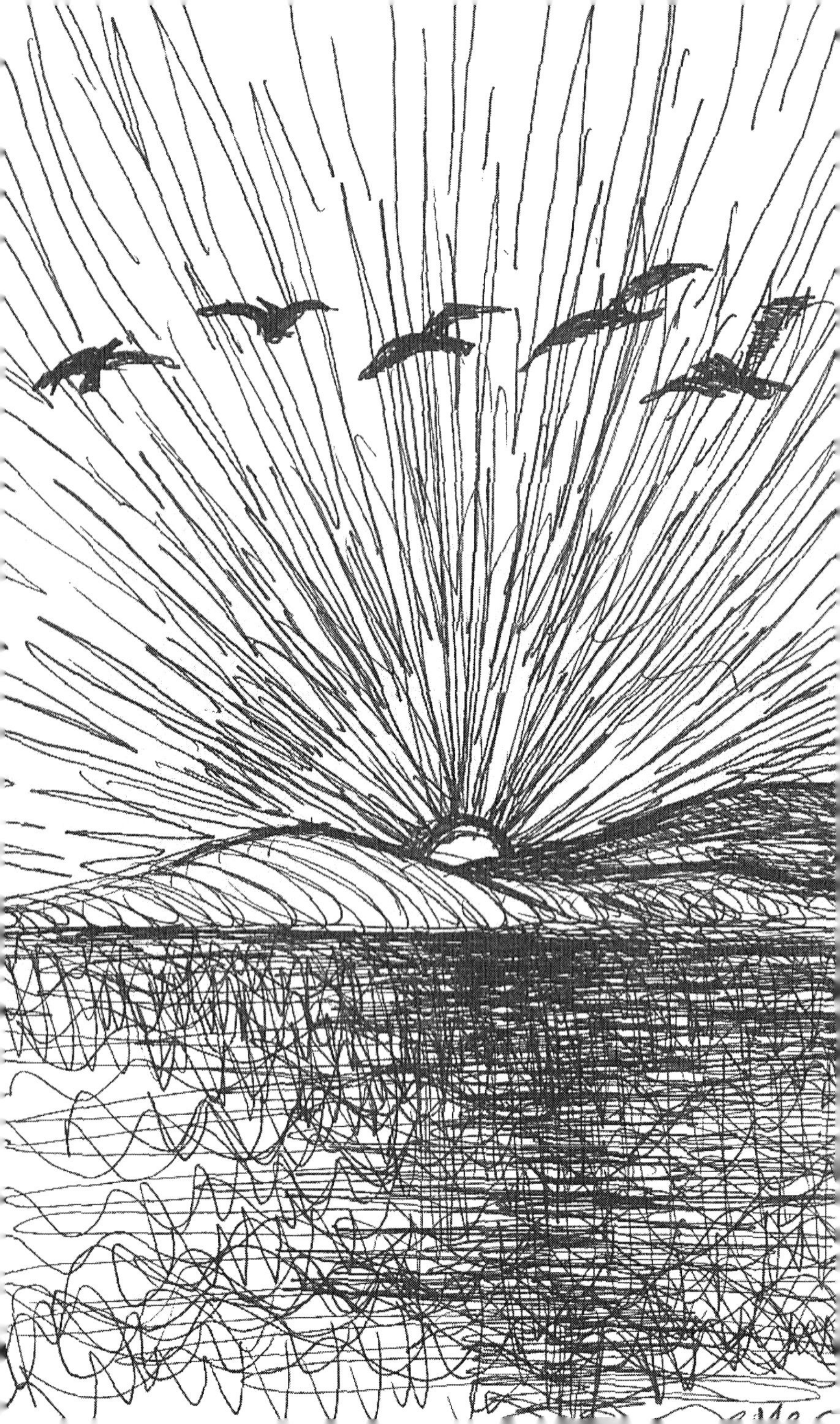

My rooster rides
On my shoulder.
My animals follow me everywhere,
Distracting, but welcome.
A cheerful clattering herd,
Eager for the next thing
To happen here
In this firm,
Unusual world.

We go, all together,
On wild adventures
That rival Tolkien's books,
Following Odysseus back home,
Going into darkness
With Gilgamesh
Under his mountain.

I write it all down
As they insist,
And in the writing
A mazy dream
Becomes real,
Regular,
A guidebook
For my waking days.

This, my animals tell me,
Is how truths are told,
How myths are made.

## Old Hen

There is no size
To a soul.

On this death day
Of her choosing
I lay a hand
On my old speckled hen.

Her feathers
Are strong silk,
Lovely
And empty.

To her I say:
Thank you
For all of your
Good years,
Good eggs,
And good attitude.

To me she says:
Fur is just a jacket
On every old
Tottering dog.
Skin is just an envelope,

Wrinkled, spotted
And luminous.

We are all
Feathered
Furred
Naked
Pieces

Of this
Same
One
Great
Love.